Advent Readings from IONA

Advent Readings from IONA

Brian Woodcock &
Jan Sutch Pickard

WILD GOOSE PUBLICATIONS

Distributed in Australia by Willow Connection Pty Ltd, Unit 4A, 3-9 Kenneth Road, Manly Vale, NSW 2093, Australia, and in New Zealand by Pleroma Christian Supplies, Higginson St., Otane 4170, Central Hawkes Bay, New Zealand.

Permission to reproduce any part of this work in Australia or New Zealand should be sought from Willow Connection.

Printed by Bell & Bain, Thornliebank, Glasgow
First Reprint 2000

The extract from Psalm 139 on the page for November 27 is © the Iona Community and the prayer is by Lea da Silva. The paragraph on the page for December 13 starting 'The rubbish dump outside one city in Brazil' is from *With All God's People: the new ecumenical prayer cycle* (p.124), 1989, WCC Publications, World Council of Churches, Geneva, Switzerland. Used by permission.

The prayer for December 23 is © Neil Paynter.

To all our friends and colleagues on Iona,
companions on this journey.

Advent Readings from IONA

Join us on a journey!

In the winter, life and work in the Iona Community's centres on the island of Iona never stop completely. A small resident group of about twelve folk go on living and working in the Abbey and MacLeod Centre, doing maintenance, training and planning for the coming season. At midwinter we welcome guests for a Christmas house party.

The whole group agreed that it would be good to have regular readings when we sat down together at table during Advent. But we couldn't find anything in print that was fresh and felt relevant.

'Let's write our own' was an inspiration that we might have regretted – except that it took us on a biblical journey through lectionary passages for the season, linking them to our own shared experience of work and worship on Iona. Two of us took alternate weeks, and occasionally days within each other's weeks. So you, the reader, like our colleagues round the table, will discern two voices, two styles, two ways of looking at the world. This little book is *from* and *for* companions – folk sharing bread and sharing a way of life. And we hope it will encourage you in your Advent journey.

Brian Woodcock, Warden   *Jan Sutch Pickard, Deputy Warden*
The Abbey and MacLeod Centre, Isle of Iona, Scotland

Advent varies in length, and there are enough readings here for any year. We have attached dates rather than days. The starting-point will always be Advent Sunday, whether as early as November 27 or as late as December 3. The last reading is for Christmas Day.

Unless otherwise stated, biblical quotations are from the New Revised Standard Version. You may wish to read the whole passage that is indicated rather than the brief extracts that we quote.

Novemb

Psalm 139: 1–4, 23–24

O God, you search me and know me.
You know my being and my doing.
From far off, you read my inmost thoughts.
You know the journeys that I take
and the places where I rest.
You know the meaning of my words before I speak…
Search me, O God, and know my heart,
test me, and know my thoughts.
See that I do not follow the wrong paths,
and guide me in the everlasting way.

This version of Psalm 139 is read regularly in the Abbey Church on Iona. It is a reminder of our journey with God, and God's closeness even when we feel very alone. Folk come to work as volunteers on Iona from many different places: Germany and Uganda, Poland and Pakistan and Palestine, Canada and the Czech Republic, Australia and New Zealand and all parts of the United Kingdom. Many have made long journeys to come here.

The journeying doesn't end, as convinced Christians, young people seeking a meaning to life, older folk at a crossroads, work together, share

,worship, and find time to talk about their lives, their experiences and their faith. And then there are the guests, who bring their own stories and their own questions. Every Saturday in the season is very busy as staff, especially the housekeepers, make the Abbey and MacLeod Centre ready for the next group of guests, *preparing* so that folk who have travelled a long way and are tired will feel welcome.

One of our volunteer housekeepers was Lea, from Brazil. She is a minister in her own church; as well as working hard as part of her team she shared in leading worship. One Sunday she preached on this psalm, seeing in it many strong messages about relationship: with ourselves, with God, with others. She did not ignore the verses where the psalmist remembers that he has enemies. She ended with a statement that seemed to come straight from the common life on Iona, and the flurry of Saturday house-keeping:

'What I find really fascinating about this psalm is that after being absolutely honest with himself and God and pouring out all his bitter feelings towards his enemies, the psalmist just seems to calm down. For me his final prayer sounds like:"Keep open the drawers of my heart and the curtains of my soul, O God. Make sure that there's no rubbish hidden under the carpets or mattresses of my inner being. Check if there is anything wrong with me, take hold of my hand and show me the right path." '

November 27

A prayer

O God, you know us better than we know ourselves –
you know my being and my doing.
In this time of Advent preparation,
help me to spring clean my life.
Help me to deepen and strengthen my relationships:
to you, to others, and to myself.
Take my hand and lead me on a journey.
Amen

November 28

Isaiah 64:1–9

O that you would tear open the heavens and come down!

Inside the house, the child was crying. His mother had gone out and locked him in! He could hear her voice, telling him not to worry, promising to come back. So why *didn't* she? Didn't she *care*? Was it something *he* had done? He felt angry, guilty and scared.

Outside, the mother was frantic. She had only slipped across the road to post a letter, but now the key had jammed. In vain she struggled with the lock. And looked for open windows. And called reassuring words through the letterbox. Till the locksmith let her in.

Only twenty minutes. But it seemed like for ever. For both of them.

A prayer

You are my maker, my watchful parent,
and even in a secular age –
when the human race has 'come of age' as they say –
I know you are there.
But there are moments when it doesn't feel like it.
Moments when I feel alone, abandoned,

shut in with my fear and anger and guilt.
And you seem distant, locked out of my life.
Only moments,
but when they come, what am I to do?

I will remember that you are only just the other side of the door,
and that, at such times, words through the letterbox really matter.
So when you tell me that you will never leave me,
that soon you are coming back,
perhaps I will feel better.
But, if you still don't come, perhaps I'll feel worse.
And when you say, 'Behold, I stand at the door and knock,'
maybe I'll realise I can do it myself,
and in utter delight I'll open the door and welcome you,
amazed that all the time it was so easy!

On the other hand,
if I can't turn the handle,
or find the lock,
what then?
Then the words through the letterbox,
the words that really matter,
will be my words.
And I will shout them loud and clear.
'What are you waiting for?' I'll scream.

'Why don't you break in?
Tear the sky apart, like the prophet said?
Break the ceiling open, like the friends of the paralysed man?
Come, as you warned, like a thief in the night,
 and force your way in?
After all, it's your home! It's where you belong!
And I'm ready, waiting, pleading
for the in-break of your kingdom!'

November 29

Revelation 22:1–7

And he said to me:
'These words are trustworthy and true,
for the Lord, the God of the spirits of the prophets
has sent his angel to show his servant
what must soon take place.
Listen! I am coming very soon!…'

Advent began in a dramatic way one year when seven potholers emerged unscathed after ten days underground, in France's largest rescue of its kind. Trapped by flooding, forty metres down, they managed to stretch their three-day supplies and survive the freezing conditions. People searching the cave system had been drilling through rocks and lowering microphones without detecting any signs of life.

Two groups of people, each listening for the other in the darkness, hoping the other was there. Neither had known for certain, but they had kept going as if life depended on it. Which it did.

'Listen! I am coming!'
Saved by the listening. And by looking.
And by not giving up.

Real humanity is sometimes buried very deep.

In our society. And within ourselves.

Sometimes we can only hope it is there;

we cannot know for certain.

But it can be found and reached, touched and healed.

And, little by little, brought back to the surface.

It is possible, if there is listening.

Listen from deep within.

And listen on behalf of others.

Whole communities can find their humanity

if a few keep on listening.

It is not always necessary to listen for words and instructions.

To listen simply for signs of life

is enough to make the connection.

But those who come to our rescue will need to listen as well.

For even God listens –

very close to us, down in the darkest places, patiently seeking us out.

Listening is our salvation. Listening, and not giving up.

We are saved by a listening God.

November 29

A prayer

I have been stumbling around in dark alleys for too long, God.
I am not expecting you to show me an easy way out;
but I am crying out for you to come and find me,
to let me know you are with me
in the darkness.

November 30
(St Andrew's Day)

John 12:20–26

Now among those who went up to worship at the festival were some Greeks. They came to Philip, who was from Bethsaida in Galilee, and said to him, 'Sir, we wish to see Jesus.' Philip went and told Andrew; then Andrew and Philip together went and told Jesus.

The student minister was about to conduct his first service. He had practised his sermon carefully and written out all his prayers. But he was still not sure. Who would be in the congregation, and what would they think of him? Would they like his illustrations and laugh at his jokes? Would they be impressed by his original interpretation of the scripture reading? How would they compare him with the student who took the service last week?

Still wondering about these things, he climbed the pulpit steps. He looked down at the waiting company. He looked down at the open Bible. There was a piece of paper below the Bible, attached to the inside of the pulpit; and on it, a brief Bible quotation. The words were simple and to the point, and shook him to the core. They said, 'Sir, we would see Jesus.'

November 30

Yes, Lord – the best we can do for anyone is take them to you.
The best we can do for ourselves, I suppose.
When our words have been said, and our knowledge aired,
if there has been no meeting with the bringer of life,
what's the point?

But some simple things elude me.
How I begin. Where you live. If I have the right.
Fine preachers, with long words from high pulpits,
haven't been able to help me work out these simple things.
But perhaps there are others who could teach me;
folk I haven't been noticing, not on public view,
who never push themselves forward, or try to impress,
or have a bad word to say about anybody.
Just good words. And kind acts. All the time.

I haven't been noticing St Andrew.
Now there was someone who didn't push himself forward.
Quite happy to go to you though, it seems.
And take others. Those Greeks. A lad with loaves and fishes.
No fuss, or false modesty, or special knowledge.
No blocking.
Just knowing where to find you, and easy in your presence.

When what people really want, and what I really need,
is to find a way to you this Advent, Lord:
save me from getting in the way,
and help me to open the door.
And if I can't do the very simple things myself,
give me the humility to ask the help
of somebody who can.

December 1

Psalm 98

Let the sea roar, and all that fills it;
the world and those who live in it.
Let the floods clap their hands;
let the hills sing together for joy
at the presence of the Lord, for he is coming
to judge the earth…

The long-awaited and well-prepared day arrived. In the morning, the royal wedding. And in the afternoon, up and down the land, hundreds of colourful street parties. In one particular street, everyone turned out. Even Fred from the corner house. The neighbours were delighted and amazed to see him there. He had become a recluse; few ever saw him these days. And no one knew his age, for he had been very old as long as anybody could remember. But there he was. Sitting at the long table, eating his jelly and ice cream with the best of them!

Delight became embarrassment, however, when he suddenly took it into his head to stand up and make a speech. To all within earshot of him it was soon apparent that today was his birthday. And that he thought this party was for him!

No one told him any different. In fact, when it came to the time for the toast to be proposed, it was to the royal family – and Fred.

December 1

Holy and gracious God,
the season of Advent is so important to me:
It's not just the parties and presents. Not for me!
What I look forward to each year,
is your coming;
your love born again, as if never before.

But save me from thinking this is just happening to me.
Or to my family.
Or to a family of like-minded people called Christians.
Remind me that Advent is about everyone,
with or without beliefs, or presents, or hangovers.

And remind me, too,
that Advent is not just for individuals,
but for the world, and everything in it;
for cultures and nations and peoples;
for justice and equality;
and for enough care of the planet to make hills sing with joy.

Remind me most of all, holy and gracious God,
that Advent is about you, and your reign over all things.
Remind me of how you changed the history of the world;
and hold time and space in your hands.

December 1

Help me to see just how big this party is!
And whatever else you do, God,
please save me from making a fool of myself
by pretending that it is my party,
or the celebration of the faithful few.

December 2

Isaiah 43:16–21

Do not remember the former things,
or consider the things of old.
I am about to do a new thing;
now it springs forth, do you not perceive it?

Whenever I went on a train journey as a child, I always insisted on having a forward-facing seat. 'Otherwise,' I explained, 'I will be ill.' But now I wonder whether my travel sickness was just an excuse. I suspect the real point was that I wanted to see where I was going. I still do. I have never been able to understand why some people choose the other seat. Why travel into the future looking only at where you have come from?

Recently it has been pointed out to me that the safest place for rail passengers is in the backward-facing seats. Personally, however, if we are going to have an accident I would rather see it coming!

A prayer

Liberator God,
Why did your exiled people look backwards so much?
Did it make them feel safer, and give them courage,
these stories of the path you made through the sea
for their ancestors to escape captivity?

Is that why they clung to the events of the past,
thinking of the good times?

It was important, of course. And understandable.
But you were wanting them to look for a new thing:
a path from their own captivity –
this time, through the wilderness.
There was so much for them to hope for now.
Not just release from Babylon.
A Messiah. A New Age.
If only they could have listened to their prophets
and looked to the future!

It happened, of course. In Bethlehem.
Some believed. Others still wait.
But here is the ironic twist:
is it not the waiting ones who look forward now;
whilst the believing ones travel through Advent
gazing two thousand years into the past?

Take us out of our backward-facing seat.
Turn us round to see what you will do.
Show us today's exiles and captives,
chains to be broken, pathways to open up.
New things, liberator God –
things that have never been written,
things we would never have thought of,
things for a New Age dawning!

December 3

Ephesians 1:3–10

[God] has made known to us his secret purpose,
in accordance with the plan which he had determined
beforehand in Christ, to be put into effect when the time is ripe:
namely, that the universe, everything in heaven and on earth,
might be brought into unity in Christ. (Revised English Bible)

There is a large housing estate in my home town that hides a secret. Before all these streets and houses were built, a bridle path led along the edge of a field to a muddy pond beneath trees. Do my childhood friends remember that muddy pond? In my imagination it is still there, somewhere beneath a row of shops.

For us it was never *just* a pond. It was an enchanted place, full of mysteries. We trawled our nets for hours, filling jars with crested newts or strange insect-like things. We tried to see below the surface, and, if the light was right, were sometimes rewarded with glimpses of a fascinating underworld. More often, though, all we saw was the sky, framed by trees. Or reflections of ourselves.

But at night, when stars and galaxies were mirrored there, the creatures were left to glide round their habitat undisturbed. We were safely tucked up in our beds then: explorers and hunters, dreaming of dinosaurs.

December 3

Christ of the cosmos, living Word,
Come to heal and save.
Come from the depths of eternity,
unfolding the purposes of God.
Come from the dawn of time,
shaping the universe:
divine expression,
mystery made known.

In your quiet hidden way,
come to heal and save.
Incognito, in our streets,
beneath the concrete, between the cracks,
behind the curtains, within the dreams,
in ageing memories, in childhood wonder,
in secret ponds, in broken hearts,
in Bethlehem stable, still small voice,
Word of God, amongst us.

Come to our divided world;
come to our fragmented lives;
come to heal and save.
In you our life is one again,
and all things come together:

each connected to the other,
each reflected in the other,
ourselves and all things living:
heaven and earth,
time and space,
the whole created universe,
in you.

Christ of the cosmos, living Word,
Come to heal and save.

December 4

Matthew 25:1–13

Keep awake therefore, for you know neither the day nor the hour.

Unkindly, they used to say of him, 'He will be late for his own funeral!' But they were wrong about him. He may not have been the world's best timekeeper, but when it really mattered he proved them wrong. First past the finishing post in the marathon! Only a local event, but important enough for a TV camera to be there. What's more, they interviewed him. He talked in glowing terms about the charity he was supporting. This was his moment of glory.

They told him it would be on the regional news, early evening. He was home just in time, switched it on, flopped into his armchair, fell asleep and missed it. It was never repeated, and no one seemed to have videoed it. But that's just typical. He will miss his own funeral, he will!

A prayer

'Keep awake,' you said, 'for you know neither day nor hour.'

But the marathon winner knew – both channel and time.
And we know. We know when we'll be celebrating Christ's birth.

And there will be no sleeping through it.
Not till after the presents and Christmas dinner, at least.

Yet your arrivals have never been so predictable and obvious.
A waiting nation sent your mother round the back to give birth.
Your favourite city didn't recognise God's moment.
Your friends travelled with you all day without realising it;
you broke bread with them, seconds before vanishing.

We catch glimpses of you when we least expect it.
And sometimes we don't. Blink, and we miss you.

Ah well – you can't win them all. Better luck next time!
It's just as well that the earth is full of your presence,
so that every meeting is a new opportunity,
a fresh encounter with you.

Only…that story about the ten young women…
You know – the five foolish ones
whose lights went out before the bridegroom arrived;
and the five selfish ones who wouldn't share their *lights…*
(I think I've got that wrong somewhere, God.
I believe they were congratulated for being wise.
I suppose the point is that there's just no substitute
for our own moments of recognition. A hard lesson!)…

Anyway, that story makes me feel a little uneasy.
Some moments, if we miss them, just can't be replayed.
So keep me awake to what you are doing.
And when. And where. And how.
Let me take nothing for granted,
nor forget you are the God of surprises.

December 5

Psalm 85:8–13

Surely salvation is at hand…
Steadfast love and faithfulness will meet,
righteousness and peace will kiss each other.

Each morning in worship we imagine justice and peace joining hands.

It is a powerful possibility. If that happened, after centuries of war and injustice, how would the world be changed? It is a memorable image, like the marathon runners who chose to cross the finishing line together, hand in hand. In the Revised English Bible justice and peace *embrace*. In the Revised Standard Version (and the AV) they *kiss*. We shouldn't lose sight of the passion – and the passionate yearning: 'Surely salvation is near.'

Sometimes waiting is very hard. When my children were babies, I carried them round with me, most of the time, as other mothers in Africa did. Sometimes I had to spend a few hours away from them. That was possible while I focused on the task in hand, the good reason for being away, the other people with whom I was spending time. But as soon as I began to travel home, mind, body, spirit were consumed with impatience, until I held them in my arms again. You must have heard the same anxiety and eagerness in the cry of a lost child, or just one left alone. At some point we've all been that child.

December 5

Is Advent a time for waiting patiently? All humanity – all creation, according to the psalmist – is in a state of intense longing. We long for God's glory, seen here as justice and peace, hand in hand, to come and dwell among us.

A prayer

God our Saviour,
walk toward us on a path of peace:
encourage us, in our loneliness and yearning,
take us in your arms and lift us up,
enable us to receive your goodness and grace,
to perceive your glory already around us,
here and now, and to believe
that justice and peace
can indeed go hand in hand.
Amen

December 6

Isaiah 61:1–3

The spirit of the Lord God is upon me,
because the Lord has anointed me;
he has sent me to bring good news to the oppressed.

This was the passage from Isaiah that Jesus read out on that Sabbath day in the synagogue, right at the beginning of his ministry…

'Doesn't he read well? One of our own young people, helping to lead worship. His mum must be proud…gives you a warm glow, doesn't it?'

Comfortable words: because we've heard them before somewhere, like folk who only go to church on weddings, funerals and Christmas Day. At one point that was our family. The vicar always asked me to read – about the shepherds-abiding-in-the-fields-keeping-watch-over-their-flocks-by-night. Which I did, relishing the words, not sure why.

Words from a long way off. What do they have to do with our lives? Any more than the story of St Nicholas, fourth-century bishop, who is said to have saved three young women from prostitution by throwing three bags of gold, for dowries, through their window one night. He became patron saint of sailors, children, merchants, pawnbrokers…and he became Santa Claus, a warm glow if ever there was one.

Stories…words…a warm glow…or real hope for real people in real need – the poor, the powerless, the captives, the mourners? Not so cosy in the real world: good news for the poor might be bad news for the well-off. Release for prisoners raises all kinds of questions for well-meaning society; our efforts alone cannot offer 'oil of gladness instead of mourners' tears'.

A prayer

The poor…the broken-hearted…
the prisoners…the mourners…
We can make it a reverent and irrelevant litany,
like counting cherry stones:
Tinker…tailor…soldier…sailor…
Rich man…poor man…beggar-man…thief…
what has this got to do with us, God?
Sailors…children…merchants…pawnbrokers…
When will it come to us?
This year…next year…sometime…never…
Yet we remember that when Jesus read these words
he added 'Today – here and now –
these words are coming true.'
Come true for us, uncomfortable God,
here and now!

December 7

Isaiah 40:1–5

In the wilderness prepare the way of the Lord,
make straight in the desert a highway for our God.

On a clear day on Iona, when we see Ben More crowned with snow
or the evening light blessing the cliffs of Burg,
when Dun I looks like the natural climax of our pilgrimage,
as though we will see the whole world from the top…
do we *want* every mountain and hill to be brought low?
We are blessed by the beauty, power and mystery
of wilderness which cuts us down to size,
and unique places cut off from the rest of the world…
Do we *really* want a highway through the desert?

How do we feel about a causeway creating a fixed link between Iona and
Mull? But then who are 'we'? 'God's glory will be revealed to every being
on earth.' It's not just our perceptions and spiritual highs that are important. It's the down-to-earth needs of our neighbours. Crossing the Sound
safely, catching the school bus, getting a wheelchair up a kerb, feeling
that the word 'family' includes you, finding the church a welcoming place:
all these are part of fullness of life.

Ireneus wrote: 'The glory of God is in human beings fully alive.' We need to be aware of what prevents life from being lived fully: the mountains, the huge physical obstacles and the barriers created by human beings, which prevent folk from continuing their pilgrimage; the wilderness which, for others, is not a place of recreation but of loss and loneliness. *When* we are aware, and *as* these are removed, then God's glory will be clear for all to see.

A prayer of Richard Baxter (17th century)

Protect us, O Lord,
during this our earthly pilgrimage
that we may seek you diligently,
walk with you lovingly and serve you faithfully;
and, having been ready to do your will in the world,
may we be eager to meet you in the glory of heaven,
through Christ our Lord.
Amen

Isaiah 40:27–31

The Creator of the ends of the earth…does not faint or grow weary.
His understanding is unsearchable. He gives power to the faint,
and strengthens the powerless.

In the year of writing, this date was the beginning of Ramadan – a period of fasting lasting for a month. Fasting, one of the 'five pillars' of Islam, may in the short term leave even young, strong people weary and faint, but is seen as a way of finding a different kind of strength, through obedience to God.

Today is also the Feast of the Immaculate Conception of the Blessed Virgin Mary. Worshipping here on Iona, we enter the debate about original sin every morning! We remind ourselves that we are made in God's image, and 'affirm God's goodness at the heart of humanity, planted more deeply than all that is wrong'. Should we let our own confused thinking about sex claim purity for Mary through a legend about her conception? Shouldn't we be celebrating her conscious, chosen 'Yes' to God?

December 8 is also the day when some Buddhists celebrate Gautama's attainment of enlightenment under the Bodhi Tree. And in the year of writing it was halfway through Hanukkah, a festival of nine days and nine candles. So it's a significant day! Different faiths celebrate the possibility that we, frail fallible human beings, can change. The passage from Isaiah, a voice from our own faith tradition, tells of God giving new strength and hope.

A prayer

O God, power of creation and constant carer,
you were there at our conception,
in the miracle of new life;
you are there in the natural and social forces
by which we are shaped and changed;
you are there in our stumbling attempts
to comprehend you, in the different expressions of our faith.
We believe that you are there, that you know and care.
In your power, may we soar as though on eagles' wings,
may we run and not feel faint,
march on and not grow weary…
in your name, eternal God.
Amen

December 9

Isaiah 41:17–20

When the poor and needy seek water
and there is none,
and their tongue is parched with thirst,
I the Lord will answer them…
I shall make the dry land springs of water.
I will plant in the wilderness the cedar…

Reflection

We live in a place with plenty of water! Sometimes it falls from a grey sky day after day. The land on which we tread is like a sponge, and burns in spate tumble down the hillsides. Water flows from our taps – clean and abundant. It is easy to take our good fortune, and water, for granted.

We also live in a place without many trees, because of the wind and the sheep. In the west of Scotland are many other places where the whole landscape was changed as landlords brought in sheep, or deer; it was not only trees that were cleared, but people. It is easy to forget past injustice.

Sometimes we become more vividly aware of injustice in the present. Hanna, who was a volunteer here on Iona, came from Bethlehem. He said, 'Water is God's gift. It comes from heaven. It falls on the earth. It makes rivers, or it sinks into the earth, and we can draw it out from wells. But now our wells on the West Bank are running dry. The Israelis have tapped into the water sources, and draw it off for their big farms and their hotels. And they sell it back to us: the water that is God's gift.'

A prayer

Here we have water, clean and abundant,
almost too much, generous God,
this water that falls as rain and is your gift.
Here we have justice, and the freedom
to drink from our own wells.
We remember those people who live in arid lands –
suffering years of drought and poor harvests –
and those whose lands are drained dry for the profit of others.
We pray for our sisters and brothers
who thirst for justice, and who hunger for peace –
who imagine peace and justice hand in hand.
We pray for a day when the thirsty land will be green with trees,
and the broken-hearted will stand tall,
like trees in your Kingdom.
Amen

December 10

Matt 11:16–19

To what will I compare this generation?
It is like children sitting in the market place
and calling to each other,
'We played the flute for you and you did not dance.
We wailed, and you did not mourn.'…

Children playing in the marketplace – but they're playing grown-up games. Games of 'He who pays the piper calls the tune', games of power, games of a World Trade Organisation and its rules, games of conformity, games of winners and losers, games of hard bargains, games of human rights and wrongs. Today, all over the world, folk are remembering the UN Declaration of Human Rights – and the many situations in which they are not honoured. In our own society we are like the children in the market-place, better at remembering our own rights, our claims on others, than our responsibilities – our calling to be aware of others and to give support. Children in Africa, who may be deprived of the rights – like education, health care, shelter – which we take for granted, spend time cheerfully, in pastures, compounds, streets and marketplaces, caring for baby brothers and sisters. From other, often materially poorer, societies we can learn the meaning of community support, of the balance between work and play, of celebration even when life is hard.

December 10

A prayer

May we learn to dance to a new tune, Jesus,
may we hear what you are playing,
and follow in your footsteps.
When you hear our clamour, like children at play –
sure that we are right and others are in the wrong:
wanting everything to go our way –
show us God's way.
Help us to recognise others' rights and our responsibilities,
help us to see what we can give up
and where we need to get involved.
When you see us caught up in self-justifying busyness,
turning celebration into a chore,
remind us that, in God's wisdom,
holy days and holidays are the same thing.
Amen

December 11

Isaiah 11:1–4a

On him the spirit of the Lord will rest:
a spirit of wisdom and understanding,
a spirit of counsel and power…
with justice he will judge the poor,
and defend the humble in the land with equity. (REB)

Reflection

The land is waiting,
waiting for the frost
to destroy the diseased plants, to cleanse the soil of pests;
waiting for the snow
to blanket and protect new shoots;
the world is waiting for the shortest day, the longest night,
for the turning of the year
and the return of light.
The people are waiting, waiting for justice –
to change their lives.
Refugees are waiting, in their in-between world,
to return home, for the past to be restored,
or for the future to be different.

The landless are trying to build a better society
starting from the *favelas* and on the rubbish tips.
People like you and me are waiting in housing estates
where problem families are dumped,
at school gates where values are confused,
waiting for health care, waiting for a loving word,
waiting on the street for the price of a cup of tea.
Victims of prejudice, hearsay, poverty, power misused –
the people are waiting
for a different kind of power to transform the land:
the gentle power of wisdom, of wonder, of God-with-us.
The people are waiting, yearning, eager, expectant…
The world is waiting.

Prayer

God of latent life and growing shoots,
we wait for you in an expectant world:
we long for your wisdom to be at work in our lives
and, with our sisters and brothers,
we yearn for your justice to be done on earth.
Amen

December 12

John 1:6–23

There was a man sent from God, whose name was John.
He came as a witness to testify to the light, so that all might believe through
him. He himself was not the light; but he came to testify to the light.

When I was a child, we had a dog which would understand but not obey. If
you pointed to something, he just looked at it; completely ignoring all
instructions to 'Fetch.'

At least that was an improvement on our previous pet, a cat. Whatever
you pointed to, the cat simply looked at the end of your finger!

A prayer

It isn't just John the Baptist who points the way,
is it, living God?
It isn't only the cry of a strange-looking man
in a remote wilderness a long time ago,
that speaks of the light coming into the world.
You surround us with signs
of the presence of Christ amongst us.
Scriptures and people, events in our lives,

art and science, song and story,
birth and death, mountain and mustard seed
are all icons –
pointing beyond themselves to a greater light,
inviting us into divine encounter and transformation.

Let us never take for granted the signposts that you give,
nor despise the lone voice or sacrificial life.
But forgive us, in this age of instant access,
when we fail to look beyond the pointer or go further.
Give us imagination to seek that which is still hidden,
patience to wait, the will to travel on,
courage to reach towards the things we cannot grasp,
humility to be led and met and taught and loved by you.
May we thank, yet never idolise, messengers you send,
but rather hear the message, and hunger for the light.

December 13

Numbers 24:1–7 & 15–17

Balaam saw that it pleased the Lord to bless Israel;
so he did not go, as at other times, to look for omens,
but set his face towards the wilderness…
So he uttered his oracle, saying:

> *'…I see him, but not now;*
> *I behold him, but not near –*
> *a star shall come out of Jacob,*
> *and a sceptre shall rise out of Israel'*

The rubbish dump outside one city in Brazil supports four to five thousand people. For many the only source of income is the garbage picking. But their potential is shown on the dump itself, where an area has been fenced off as a garden. There people have planted seeds found in the garbage. Corn, beans, pumpkins grow there; to feed their families and as a sign of hope.

A prayer

He set his face towards the wilderness, and saw the stars.
He planted seeds of hope.
How was it possible, in such a place, God?

The wilderness was exodus territory,
but hardly an escape into paradise!
Endless wandering round endless scrub-land,
longing to be back in Egypt.
Where are the seeds of hope in that, God?
Yet it was there that they nurtured their dream
of a promised land, of a future nation.
Of a rising star. Someday.
A dream to keep them going.
In the wilderness.

The wilderness is a Brazilian rubbish dump.
Home for hundreds. Stateless population.
And seeds of hope there, too.
Do they have a dream, God – a rising star someday –
to keep them going in the wilderness?

Wilderness all around. Wilderness within.
Broken lives, broken world, broken hearts.
Soulless shadow side. Pretend it isn't there!
Yet if we dare set our faces towards it –
risk despair, see stars –
will we find seeds of hope there?
Plant them in the broken earth?
Nurture a dream to keep us going?

A vision for our world?
A rising star?
In the wilderness?
Will we, living God?

December 14

1 Corinthians 1:18–2:7

'I will destroy the wisdom of the wise,
and bring to nothing the cleverness of the clever.'
Where is your wise man now?… (Revised English Bible)

'Where are the Wise Men *now?*' demanded Mrs Alexander.

She didn't seem to realise she was quoting the Bible. She didn't seem to *care.* The nativity play rehearsal was all that mattered. Originally, her hope had been that she might get through it without having to raise her voice to the class; but she had given up that idea long since. For some reason it had proved impossible to keep all the children together. She had used up more energy getting them to sit down and wait than getting them to stand up and perform.

The Wise Men had been the worst – forever wandering off. They had had to wait longest, because they only came on at the end. Every time she turned round, they had gone again. 'Looking for Golden Frankenstein to bring to the stable,' they had said. Or, 'Making crowns for our heads.' And Mrs Alexander had explained yet again that they didn't *need* props and costumes and stables, because this was not a dress rehearsal; that all they needed was imagination and patience. But patience was what Mrs Alexander was now running out of herself.

Which is why, when their turn finally came and they had disappeared *again,* her words 'Where are the Wise Men *now?*' had sounded rather like an explosion.

Tom, who was one of them, came into view at the back of the hall. Alone. But his reply showed little grasp of the gravity of the situation, little concern for the tableau that was poised there – Mary and Joseph, shepherds and sheep, angels and Mrs Alexander. His reply conveyed complete innocence, as if he and his two companions were doing all they could to help things along.

'Please Miss,' he shouted from the back of the hall, 'we're looking for the baby!'

Neither Tom nor Mrs Alexander seemed to realise he was quoting the Bible.

A prayer

Where are the Wise Ones now, God?
Last to enter a nativity scene that has not yet begun to assemble.
So perhaps it's a little premature to ask.

But they must be on their way;
already wondering what to look for, where to search, who to ask.
Will they blunder in again, from their alien culture,
stirring up a hornets' nest with innocent enquiries about a baby,
while the tableau looks on helplessly?

Who are the Wise Ones, anyway?
Herod or magi? Innkeeper or donkey?
Politician or preacher, pop star or pauper?
Primary school teacher or three bored kids at the back?
In a world where people keep falling off pedestals, God,
where do we find the Wise Ones;
and where is the beginning of wisdom?

December 15

Luke 7:18–23

They said, 'John the Baptist has sent us to you to ask,
"Are you the one who is to come, or are we to wait for another?" '

The guests were starting to arrive for the centenary celebration, and the deaconess was standing at the door waiting to greet the new mayor. She wondered how she would recognise him, but was assured that other people wouldn't be wearing chains round their necks.

When a chauffeur-driven car pulled up at the specially coned-off area, she came forward and greeted the impressive-looking gentleman who emerged, and led him into the building. But after being introduced to one or two people, he tactfully informed her that he was not the new mayor! She apologised profusely, only grateful that she had not already ushered him to a VIP seat.

Meanwhile, however, she had missed the real mayor. He had passed her in the corridor, but how could she have known? Not only was he chainless; he looked so *ordinary*! Furthermore, he had *walked* to the church, and come in at the back door. It was the caretaker who pointed him out to her. 'Yes, I know Bert,' he said. 'I used to do the soup run with him.'

December 15

Jesus, are you the one?
It is hardly surprising that people missed your coming
when even John the Baptist wasn't sure.

They were expecting such a different kind of messiah.
The unmistakable kind.
Chauffeur-driven, on a VIP throne, with a gold chain.
How could anyone be expected to know who you were
when you came in at the back, looking ordinary?

There were plenty who did recognise you, of course:
the blind man who cried, 'Son of David, have pity!',
the disturbed one who screamed, 'Stay away!',
the woman who touched the hem of your coat,
the folk who knew you from the soup run.
But are you the one, Jesus? We still have to ask.
In a world of paths and promises, how can we be sure?
Your reply is your work amongst the sick and oppressed.
'Decide for yourselves!' you say –
as if it isn't the doctrines, or even the miracles,
but the company you keep and the priorities you hold,
and the kingdom of possibilities and joy
you unpack amid our ordinariness.

So help us to be on the look-out for your coming,
as the people and events crowd in.
Open our eyes to see you in the guise of friend and stranger.
Whatever the path, wherever the place,
however you come to us,
may there be recognition.
And joyous welcoming.

December 16

Isaiah 54:1–10

Sing, O barren one who did not bear;
burst into song and shout,
you who have not been in labour!
…my steadfast love shall not depart from you,
and my covenant of peace shall not be removed.

Reflection

She was childless – but in no way was she barren.
It was just the way life had worked out:
no life-long partner, though several strong and lasting friendships.
No children, though years of congratulating and encouraging
folk of her own generation who did become parents.
Yes, there was a sense of what might have been,
month by month her body had prepared for the possibility of new life –
she knew it was in working order.
But the right relationship, the right time, never happened.
She believed that she would have been a good mother
so sometimes, in low moments, she felt incomplete.
And yet…no one would have called her barren.

To her friends' children she was an adoptive aunt:
source of surprises when they were little,
a wise listener and vital ally as they struggled through adolescence.
She was often much easier to talk to than their own parents.
She offered unconditional love.
How could she be called barren? Her adult friendships were creative:
in them she and others grew through a sharing of interests
and care for each other.
She was a teacher: all over the world now
there are people who write to tell her how much they owe to her:
insights that changed their lives, confidence to be themselves,
courage to take new directions.
All her life she has been a source of life.
She is childless, but she is not barren.
And God is not finished with her yet.

A prayer

Yes, God, we will sing, even through our tears,
because we believe that you value our lives, chaotic or incomplete,
and through us are bringing your new life into being.
We feel your compassion, we respond to your covenant,
we know your steadfast love. Yes, we will sing!
Amen

1 Thessalonians 5:12–24

May God himself, the God of peace,
make you holy through and through,
and keep you sound in spirit, soul and body,
free from any fault when our Lord Jesus Christ comes.
(Revised English Bible)

People travel great distances to find holiness. Some even come to Iona.

There is the story of a boy who lived in an isolated house on a hill. A God-forsaken place for a young man. But one thing fascinated him. Each night he would look out into the darkness and see a light. It was far away on a hilltop, but this sign of life gave him hope.

One day he decided to go in search of it. It was a long and lonely walk, and it was already dark before he reached the outskirts of a town. Tired and hungry, he knocked at the first door he came to, and explained his search for the mysterious light that had always given him hope.

'I know it!' replied the woman who had answered the door. 'It gives me hope as well.' And she pointed back in the direction from which he had come. There, on the horizon, was a single light shining. A sign of life in the darkness. The light from his own house.

A prayer

God of light,
in this age of spiritual quests,
open our eyes to what we already have.
And teach us that the most important sacred place
is within.

We may not feel very holy. Or even want to be.
We may have known people whose sense of their own holiness
was enough to put us off religion for life.
Surely we don't have to be like that
at the coming of Jesus Christ!

Wasn't Jesus more interested in wholeness than in being holy?
Perhaps that's the kind of 'holiness' Paul was talking about, God:
'wholeness', with a 'w',
soundness of spirit, soul and body, as he put it;
of the whole person, and the whole people.

That I can take, living God.
But I don't know if it can take me!
My kind of holiness is 'hole-iness', with an 'e' in the middle –
which means 'full of holes'.
Hardly the soundness and faultlessness Paul had in mind.

But then I think about the ordinary folk and rejected folk Jesus called;
about how he said it was the sick and not the healthy who needed him;
about his story of the Pharisee and publican praying together.
And I wonder whether a few holes in our holiness might be allowed.

Teach us, God of light,
that we do not have to be faultless before the Lord Jesus will come;
that we do not have to pretend to be anything we are not;
that when he comes he will help us to be what he wants us to be;
and that what he wants to give us is not religion, but our humanity.
Grant us, then, the holiness of being fully human;
and, if it be your will,
turn the holes within us into sacred spaces.

December 18

Isaiah 7:10–14

Therefore the Lord himself will give you a sign. Look, a young woman is with child and shall bear a son, and shall name him Immanuel.

The convent was in the south-east of England, but there was no mistaking the painting on the wall. That single doorway with its rounded stone Norman arch. Within it the heavy wooden door, slightly ajar. Above, strangely overlapping, columns supporting later Gothic arches.

'It's Iona Abbey,' I remarked knowledgeably.

'Yes,' replied the sister. 'I love this picture. I use it to meditate. I think of how the door opens on to that beautiful island, and it is as if I am there.'

Again I aired my knowledge. 'But that is the door into the sacristy,' I said. 'It doesn't lead outside.'

The moment the words were out I wanted to take them back. But she simply looked at me, and said quietly, 'Well, it does for *me*.'

A prayer

What is truth, God? Imagination or reality?
The magic of an island or the correct position of a door?
I prefer magic, God – especially at this time of year.

Christmas magic! Expectation and expectancy!
Ancient prophecies coming true
as, once again, the story unfolds.
A virgin becoming pregnant and having a son
and calling him Immanuel.
And Isaiah already making the announcement
over seven hundred years before the event.
Your sign to the shepherds. Your sign to the whole people.

But if the sign was meant for King Ahaz, and not shepherds…
if Isaiah didn't actually say 'virgin', but 'young woman'…
…is this magical time just magic, God?
Events glamorised? Scriptures twisted? History rewritten?
If we can't rely on the prophets' words,
what about the Christmas story itself?
Can we ever know the truth?

Yes, we can. We do.
You are the Truth: we can know you!
But you make yourself known in such disconcerting ways:
through fact and fantasy and faulty memory,
through faithless nations and frightened disciples,
through human frailty and fallibility,
even through people like us.

Come, share our humanness, Immanuel, God-with-us.
Use our pictures, our imagination, to take us through the door.
Use our knowledge and ignorance to explore the view beyond.
Use our stories and customs to tell the deeper things:
That we can know you. That you know us.
That love is born again.

December

Romans 16:25–27

Let us give glory to God! He is able to make you stand firm in your faith, according to the Good News I preach about Jesus Christ and according to the revelation of the secret truth which was hidden for long ages in the past. Now, however, that truth has been brought out into the open… (GNB)

A flight of fancy

Tertius, who was taking dictation, put down his pen, and looked at Paul. Was that all? And what were the Christians in Rome going to make of it? These circular letters were always tricky, and yet really they were the only solution to the season of goodwill, and all the people who expected a greeting. Thank goodness cards hadn't been invented. On the other hand, a word processor would have been handy – but that would have meant waiting almost 2000 years. It was all very well for Timothy, Lucius, Jason and Sosipater – they just added 'Say hello from us, too' – or words to that effect. But Paul wanted to say more. He had a message for particular people in a particular place (the Christians in Rome) – but it was also good news for everyone.

'That's all,' said Paul, 'I'll just sign off: 'To the only God, who alone is all-wise, be glory through Jesus Christ for ever! Amen.'

Paul's letters are communications between adult communities. Yet the glory and mystery he celebrates are sometimes beyond all our careful words. God's 'secret truth' was revealed to us in the Incarnation – in the midst of human life – an unexpected pregnancy, and the mess and wonder of a child being born to people on the move in a world of corruption, conflict and confusion. The abstractions of theological language and the blandness of our Christmas circulars cannot do justice to the down-to-earth nature of what happened two thousand years ago – and is still happening today. God's wisdom does not set God apart, but takes human form.

A prayer

Immanuel, God with us,
help us to stand firm in our faith
and to go on discovering what the Good News is for us, here and now.
Help us not to take refuge in words:
other people's words, abstractions,
bland formulations, churchy jargon.
Surprise us with your poetry,
your pictures, which are beyond words,
your living letters, which are people,
your signs, which are at once here-and-now
and belong to all places, all times, all people,
your wisdom, which can only be understood by the child in us.
God of surprises, God with us.
Amen

December 20

Psalm 113:2–9

From the rising of the sun to its setting
may the Lord's name be praised. (REB)

A reflection

Of course that doesn't give us very long – from sunrise to sunset. What's that at the moment? 9 am to 4 pm? We are reaching the shortest day. At this time of year it's easy to imagine the monks of Columba's time, using the precious daylight for necessary chores like fetching water, milling the barley, preparing meals, crossing the Sound in little boats, building their beehive huts: the demanding common task. They must have valued the daylight for the work of copying and illuminating manuscripts, where accuracy and intricate artistry were both important. They praised God at sunrise and sunset, and gathered to worship God in the long watches of the night, too. But of course they were worshipping God in everything they did.

In the same way we too are worshipping God 'from the rising of the sun to its setting', whether that's a brief, bleak winter's day like this one, or one of those Iona midsummer nights to which we look forward, when it never gets completely dark, when the sunset's afterglow moves round

the northern horizon until it becomes the brightness of the dawn sky.
God is present in the awesome power of creation, the strong sun, the
mysterious moon, an infinity of stars; towering mountains and stormy
seas. But God is also there in the detail: frost crystals, a robin's song, the
way we spend our days.

God sees the sparrow fall and the child born in a refugee camp; knows
the needs of those who live on the edge, values those on whom the
world has given up. The psalm praises a God who 'is seated on high', but
who 'raises the poor from the dust…and makes them sit with princes.'

A prayer

God, what are you like?
Like the looming presence of a mountain,
of Ben More looking over the shoulder of Burg,
watching our tiny island from far off?
And yet you are a God who comes close,
who finds us when we are lost,
lifts us up when we think we can sink no lower;
a caring God who takes us by the hand
and sits us at a table full of friends.
You make space for each of us in our emptiness,
you remind us again of our goodness – and our creativity.
So we glorify you by being fully ourselves, fully alive.
Amen

December 21

Luke 1:26–38

The angel said to her, 'Do not be afraid Mary,
for God has been gracious to you;
you will conceive and give birth to a son,
and you are to give him the name Jesus…
'I am the Lord's servant,' said Mary, 'may it be as you have said.' (REB)

A reflection

Two children were talking about angels.

Adam said: 'An angel is a bit like a tooth fairy…but it does not collect teeth. An angel is a good person…but maybe it's not. An angel has two wings and it wears pink…but it might not…'

Kirsty was sure about some things: 'An angel is a little thing that flies and wears no shoes. Sometimes it is invisible, but all the time it goes about doing good things and making people happy… Oh yes and it also has a harp, then it can sing little songs to help people forget their troubles…'

Adam and Kirsty's words were recorded in the Angel of the North project based in Gateshead. It's easy to imagine the Sunday School pictures and stained glass windows that inspired the wings, the harp, the pink robes…

But did Gabriel look anything like that? How do we imagine an archangel? And what does Gabriel have in common with the tooth fairy? *Did* God's messenger really sing a little song to help Mary forget her troubles? Quite the opposite – the message itself was deeply troubling… perplexing, frightening. Mary cried out: 'How can this be?'

But in the end she said, 'Let it be.'

A prayer

How can it be, God, that you chose Mary?
She was just a village girl, in an obscure part of the world
which never quite made the headlines.
How can it be that you sent this poor woman an angel
to terrify and confuse her
with news that turned her world upside down?
How can it be that Gabriel, beating great wings,
filling the house with light, could say, 'Do not be afraid'?
How can it be that she was no longer afraid
and talked with the angel, as with an equal?
How can it be that she said 'yes' to you, God?
I do not understand, but I am encouraged:
if you send me an angel
may I not be afraid. May I say 'yes'.
Amen

December 22

Luke 1:39–45

When Elizabeth heard Mary's greeting, the baby leapt in her
womb. And Elizabeth was filled with the Holy Spirit and
exclaimed with a loud cry, 'You are the most blessed of all
women, and blessed is the fruit of your womb!'

A reflection

The first time I felt my first child kicking inside me was at a Johnny
Dankworth concert. Maybe the rhythm woke him up and he began to
dance. Maybe it was because for once I wasn't rushing about, so wasn't
too busy to notice a new and subtle sensation. Maybe I was more receptive, along with the new life I was carrying.

Elizabeth must have been more receptive to God's different ways of
working. After all, she was very old – though it's hard for us to know what
'very old' would mean in another culture and time – and yet had become
pregnant. Her equally elderly husband, who wasn't usually stuck for a
word to say, hadn't spoken to her for six months – but then he hadn't
spoken to anyone. She was waiting to see what it all meant. And then
Mary, her young cousin, came to visit – and as they spoke to each other,
Elizabeth's unborn child leapt to life and began kicking. Why?

For Elizabeth this was a sign that in this homely meeting between two mothers-to-be there was also an encounter with God. John was the baby who would be born first. Was this the first time he pointed to 'the one who was to come after'? Was he dancing for joy at the presence of the Messiah? In which case, why didn't he recognise the Messiah when Jesus came for baptism? And why did John later send his disciples to ask, 'Are you the Christ?'

These are questions asked in hindsight. Today we celebrate the far-seeing of the child who danced before he was born, and the perceptive-ness of the woman who was more than a womb: the prophet Elizabeth.

A prayer

God who comes close,
help us to perceive your presence
in ourselves, in others.
Help us to speak out, and affirm it;
help us to keep quiet, and reflect on the mystery.
And, when the time is right,
help us to dance with joy.
Amen

December 23

Luke 1:46–56

Mary said, 'My soul magnifies the Lord,
and my spirit rejoices in God my Saviour
for he has looked with favour on the lowliness of his servant…'

A reflection

Mary called herself God's servant, God's handmaid, a down-to-earth, useful role. There is a story about a school nativity play where Joseph introduced himself as 'the *handyman* of the Lord', which seems very appropriate given that he earned a living as a joiner. In terms of our community here, Joseph worked in maintenance, and Mary in house-keeping…and Gabriel was probably a programme worker…

Mary kept house for God in another sense. She welcomed the Creator of earth and sea and sky as a new-created being, an embryo beginning to grow in the shelter of her body. She wondered at the angel's message, and kept it to herself, while she bore the disapproval of the neighbours and the distress of Joseph. She carried and cradled the growing child from Nazareth to Judaea, and back again; to the well, to the vegetable garden, to the market, about her daily work, until the couple set out for the census in Bethlehem. She refused to be ashamed but she was filled with amazement, and she celebrated God's power and mercy 'from generation to generation'. Just as John danced before he was born, and Elizabeth cried out with joy, so Mary sang in her heart.

She sang about liberation, and about a world turned upside down, about the rich sent away empty, and the poor and hungry filled with good things. She knew at first hand what this meant. And, ever since, her story and her song have given hope to the poor, the rejected, people on the margins. Not to mention housekeepers and handymen.

A prayer by Neil Paynter

We praise you, O God,
in Christ you came to turn the world upside down,
to bring down the powerful and to lift up the lowly;
in Christ you came to turn the tables,
to fling away vain idols and to scatter the proud;
in Christ you came to stir up a revolution of love:
to feed the hungry, to clothe the poor,
to give sight to the blind, to set the captives free;
in Christ you came to proclaim your Kingdom here on earth –
to turn the world downside up.
We praise you!
Amen

December 24

Luke 1:78–79

By the tender mercy of our God,
the dawn from on high will break upon us,
to give light to those who sit in darkness
and in the shadow of death,
to guide our feet into the way of peace.

Comment

This is part of the song of Zechariah. At last he was able to speak –
released from his nine-month silence in the moment that Elizabeth
named their child 'John' and he affirmed her choice. She had intuitively
chosen the name the angel gave. Zechariah's silence had been part of the
shock of meeting an angel. It was also an expression of his incredulity –
about becoming a father, about God's plan and God's way of putting it
into action. Maybe he saw 'being dumbstruck' as a punishment for lack of
faith. Certainly, having no voice disempowered him. He was a priest. How
could he perform his role without a voice? He was a man. How could he
let his wife speak for him? When at last 'his mouth was opened and his
tongue freed', his first words praised God.

How can we praise God, who has given us the gift of language, in this time and place? If we went out tonight, to stand by St Martin's Cross, it would be clear that Zechariah's song – about giving light to those in darkness – is still relevant to us now.

A prayer-reflection

For millennia
the light of the stars has travelled.
For a thousand years
this cross has withstood the winds.
For a hundred years of war
wave has followed wave
while people walking in darkness
have longed for peace.
But before our time, before all time:
in the beginning, the Word.

In this moment
the snowflake, a perfect crystal, is formed and falls.
In this moment
the snowdrop, in the dark earth, waits for the returning sun.
In this moment
a child is born, a life begins, blooms…
And in this time, our time, God's time:
in each beginning, the Word.
Amen

December 25
Christmas Day

Luke 2:8–20

This will be a sign for you: you will find a child
wrapped in bands of cloth and lying in a manger.

Years ago, on a train journey, I found myself in conversation with a man who told me he was redesigning a town. He had spent the last couple of days wandering the back alleys and forgotten places of that community. At one point he had spotted some young lads disappearing through a gap between the bent railings of a fence. Following them into the under-growth, he had found himself in a clearing amongst a group of children. It was their secret den. Their only question: 'How did you find us?'

He said to me: 'I believe that if I am to plan a town, I must do so from the *inside*. I must find out what makes it tick and how it keeps its secrets. Any new development must be in tune with this. There must be the space and freedom for its people to create their own secret dens. Otherwise the town will lose its soul.'

December 25

God of good news,
today you begin again to reshape our lives and communities.
You do not start from the outside, but from within.
You begin in the hidden place.
Behind the inn. Before the marriage. At the wrong time.
You invite a handful of guests into your company.
Shepherds. Local children perhaps. Maybe some animals.
You join the community of the invisible ones.
The homeless and hopeless. Refugees, fleeing a tyrant king.
Later, you find fisherfolk. And a tax collector. More children.
The small. The unimportant. The forgotten. The frightened.
These are the people you choose,
as little by little you start sharing
the secrets of a kingdom that will change the whole world.
From within. From the hidden place.

God of good news:
as we celebrate worldwide the tidings of your birth,
as we set the heavens echoing with angel songs,
as we contemplate new year and pray for peace on earth...
remind us of the hidden places, of the forgotten people,
of the starting-points and the time it takes,
of the pace of the slowest and the dreams of the children
and the human scale and the soul of our towns
and the freedom to create secret dens.

Remind us that the great joy promised to the whole people
starts with those who need it most, in places where they hide.
Remind us, with all our seasonal cheer and tinsel,
that some people are left out in the cold;
that it is there, with them, that you are being born into the world again;
that it is there, through them, that you will change the world.

God of good news,
help us to find you again
in the hidden place.
Amen

The Iona Community

The Iona Community is an ecumenical Christian community, founded in 1938 by the late Lord MacLeod of Fuinary (the Revd George MacLeod DD) and committed to seeking new ways of living the Gospel in today's world. Gathered around the rebuilding of the ancient monastic buildings of Iona Abbey, but with its original inspiration in the poorest areas of Glasgow during the Depression, the Community has sought ever since the 'rebuilding of the common life', bringing together work and worship, prayer and politics, the sacred and the secular in ways that reflect its strongly incarnational theology.

The Community today is a movement of over 200 Members, around 1,500 Associate Members and about 700 Friends. The Members – women and men from many backgrounds and denominations, most in Britain, but some overseas – are committed to a rule of daily prayer and Bible reading, sharing and accounting for their use of time and money, regular meeting and action for justice and peace.

The Iona Community maintains three centres on Iona and Mull: Iona Abbey and the MacLeod Centre on Iona, and Camas Adventure Camp on the Ross of Mull. Its base is in Community House, Glasgow, where it also supports work with young people, the Wild Goose Resource and Worship Groups, a bimonthly magazine (Coracle) and a publishing house (Wild Goose Publications).

For further information on the Iona Community please contact:

The Iona Community
Pearce Institute,
840 Govan Road
Glasgow G51 3UU
T. 0141 445 4561; F. 0141 445 4295
e-mail: ionacomm@gla.iona.org.uk
web: www.iona.org.uk

Dandelions & Thistles

Biblical meditations from the Iona Community

Jan Sutch Pickard (Ed)

A beautiful, illustrated book presenting Bible stories in the form of radical, thought-provoking meditations by various contributors. These monologues, scripts and poems give profound and sensitive messages in a simple and direct style accessible to all, making them perfect for use in group or worship situations or for individual reflection.

Contributors include: Jan Sutch Pickard Kate McIlhagga John L. Bell Joy Mead Ruth Burgess Yvonne Morland David Osborne Kathy Galloway Norman Shanks John Davies Anna Briggs

1999 · 96pp · 1 901557 14 6 · £9.99

Meditations from the Iona Community

Ian M Reid

Biblical meditations from a former leader of the Iona Community, published to commemorate the sixtieth anniversary of the Community in 1998. Ian Reid died before this project was completed, so this book is also an expression of the Community's love and thanksgiving for his life. A large-format book with illustrations.

1998 · 96pp · 1 901557 02 2 · £8.99

Cloth for the Cradle

Worship resources and readings for Advent,
Christmas and Epiphany
Wild Goose Worship Group

This rediscovery of the stories of Christ's birth through adult eyes
contains much to reflect on individually and to use in group and worship
situations. The material is drawn from the work of the Wild Goose Worship
Group whose innovative style of worship is widely admired and imitated.

1998 · 152pp · 1 901557 01 4 · £10.99

The Pattern of Our Days

Liturgies and resources for worship
from the Iona Community
Edited by Kathy Galloway

This inspiring anthology, reflecting the life and witness of the Iona
Community, is intended to encourage creativity in worship.

Liturgies: Pilgrimage and journeys • Healing • Acts of witness and
dissent • A sanctuary and a light • **Resources:** Beginnings and endings
of worship • Short prayers • Prayers for forgiveness • Words of faith •
Thanksgiving: Concern • Litanies and responses • Cursings and blessings
• Reflections, readings and meditations.

1996 · 192pp · 0 947988 76 9 · £7.99

*To receive a copy of our latest catalogue, please contact
Wild Goose Publications, Unit 16, Six Harmony Row, Glasgow G51 3BA.
Tel. 0141 440 0985 Fax 0141 440 2338 e-mail: admin@wgp.iona.org.uk*